Hearing

First published in paperback 2011,
by Evans Brothers Limited
2A Portman Mansions
Chiltern Street
London W1U 6NR

Produced for Evans Brothers Limited by
White-Thomson Publishing Ltd

Printed by Everbest in China
July 2011, job number (CAG1678)
Printed on chlorine-free paper from sustainably managed sources.

Educational consultant: Sue Palmer MEd FRSA FEA
Project manager: Katie Dicker
Picture research: Amy Sparks
Design: Balley Design Limited
Creative director: Simon Balley
Designer/Illustrator: Andrew Li

The activities in this book are designed to be used at the discretion of the pre-school
practitioner, teacher or parent/guardian. The publisher shall not be liable for any
accidents, losses or malpractices arising from or relating to these activities.

British Library Cataloguing in Publication Data

Dicker, Katie
   Hearing. - (My senses) (Sparklers)
   1. Hearing - Pictorial works - Juvenile literature
   I. Title
   612.8'5

ISBN: 978 0 2375 4447 8

Contents

Listen out!

Wh-i-sss-p-er

We use our **ears** to listen.

Do **YOU** have a **secret** to tell?

6

What sounds do
you like to hear?

Animal ears

What was that?

Animals listen for **sounds** of danger.

Dolphins can hear
very high sounds.

Weather Sounds

splish

splash

Raindrops make a **splashing** sound.

What other weather sounds can you think of ?

crunch, crunch!

Are **YOU** ready to make some loud sounds?

toot!

twang!

squeeze!

Which instrument would you like to play?

13

Look after your ears

We cover our **ears** when noises get TOO LOUD!

Sam wears a hearing aid. It makes sounds clearer.

15

We listen on the **telephone** to people who are **far** away.

17

Sound Warnings

NEE-NAAR!

LOUD sounds tell us to LOOK OUT!

Graaaaarrrr!

Can you make a **noise** like an **angry** bear?

19

Daily sounds

brish, brush

Think of all the **sounds** you **hear**,

from when you **wake** up...

Notes for adults

Sparklers books are designed to support and extend the learning of young children. The **Food We Eat** titles won a Practical Pre-School Sliver Award, the **Body Moves** titles won a Practical Pre-School Gold Award and the **Out and About** titles won the 2009 Practical Pre-School Gold Overall Winner Award. The books' high-interest subjects link in to the Early Years Foundation Stage curriculum and beyond. Find out more about Early Years and reading with children from the National Literacy Trust (www.literacytrust.org.uk).

Themed titles
Hearing is one of four **Senses** titles that explore the five senses of sight, touch, smell, taste and sound. The other titles are:

Seeing   **Tasting and Smelling**   **Touching and Feeling**

Areas of learning
Each **Senses** title helps to support the following Foundation Stage areas of learning:
Personal, Social and Emotional Development
Communication, Language and Literacy
Mathematical Development
Knowledge and Understanding of the World
Physical Development
Creative Development

Making the most of reading time
When reading with younger children, take time to explore the pictures together. Ask children to find, identify, count or describe different objects. Point out colours and textures. Allow quiet spaces in your reading so that children can ask questions or repeat your words. Try pausing mid-sentence so that children can predict the next word. This sort of participation develops early reading skills.

Follow the words with your finger as you read. The main text is in Infant Sassoon, a clear, friendly font designed for children learning to read and write. The labels and sound effects add fun and give the opportunity to distinguish between levels of communication. Where appropriate, labels, sound effects or main text may be presented phonically. Encourage children to imitate the sounds.

As you read the book, you can also take the opportunity to talk about the book itself with appropriate vocabulary such as "page", "cover", "back", "front", "photograph", "label" and "page number".

You can also extend children's learning by using the books as a springboard for discussion and further activities. There are a few suggestions on the facing page.

Pages 4–5: Sounds of nature

Make some shakers by filling jam jars with different materials, such as rice, marbles, paper clips, seeds and cotton wool. Ask children to try out each shaker in turn. Which is the loudest shaker? Which is the quietest? Ask the children to place the shakers in order of loudness.

Pages 6–7: Listen out!

Children may enjoy playing 'Chinese whispers'. Ask the children to sit quietly in a circle. Give one child a piece of paper with a short message on it. Ask them to whisper the message to their neighbour. As each child listens and whispers, the message may become altered. Compare the final outcome with the original message. Explain to children the importance of listening.

Pages 8–9: Animal ears

Cut out photographs of animals from wildlife magazines. Cut off the ears from each animal and ask children to match the animals with their ears. Encourage the children to think about what the animals use their ears for and put a collage of the 'matched' animals on the wall.

Pages 10–11: Weather sounds

Make a recording of different weather sounds such as wind, rain, hail, thunder and walking on snow. Collect photographs from magazines depicting each type of weather, too. Ask children to identify the different recorded sounds and to match them to an appropriate photograph.

Pages 12–13: Making music

Take a selection of empty glass bottles and fill them with various quantities of water. Ask children to tap each bottle in turn. Which makes the highest sound? Which makes the lowest? Ask the children to place the bottles in order of their pitch. Children may also enjoy making a tune by tapping the glass bottles.

Pages 14–15: Look after your ears

Children may enjoy learning some basic sign language (for example, see http://www.under5s.co.uk/signs.htm). You could also encourage children to think about a sign language of their own, and how they might be able to help someone who is deaf.

Pages 16–17: Say hello

Ask children to think about all the different ways that they hear people talking when they are far away. Examples may include television, radio, telephone or a microphone. Children may enjoy acting out one of these examples by standing on different sides of a screen, and talking to each other remotely.

Pages 18–19: Sound warnings

Ask children to think about the different types of sound warnings they have at home or in their classroom. Discuss what these sounds are used for. Examples may include an alarm clock, doorbell, microwave buzzer, oven temperature buzzer, cooking timer or kettle whistle/click.

Pages 20–21: Daily sounds

Encourage children to think about all the sounds they do and don't like. What do different sounds make them feel like? What is it about the sounds that they do or don't like – their pitch, their loudness, their continuity? Ask the children to draw a picture or collage illustrating some of their favourite sounds.

Index

Picture acknowledgements:
Corbis: cover, 13 guitar (Sean Justice), 6, 11 (Don Mason), 12 (M.A.Pushpa Kumara/epa), 13 accordion (Sean Justice), 14 (Redlink), 17 woman (Jagdish Agarwal), 19 (DLILLC), 20 (Sandra Seckinger/zef); **Getty Images:** 7 (Imagemore); **IStockphoto:** cover grass (Dean Turner), cover sky (Judy Foldetta); **Photolibrary:** 4 monkey, 10 (Simon Marcus), 15 (Bernhard J Widmann); **Shutterstock:** 2-3 compact discs (Kulish Viktoria), 4-5 rainforest (Paul Zizka), 4 toucan (Chris Hill), 5 lion (Kristian Sekulic), 5 snake (Maria Dryfhout), 8 (Misha Shiyanov), 9 (Kristian Sekulic), 13 recorder (Jules Studio), 16 (digitalskillet), 17 boy (Arvind Balaraman), 17 globe (Emanuel), 18 (Ramon Berk), 21 (Glenda M. Powers), 22-23 keyboard (Georgy Markov), 24 keyboard (Georgy Markov).